# NUMBERS, SHAPES AND ADDITION

# Numbers, Shapes and Addition

Erika Burton

# CONTENTS

Dedication . . . . . . . . . . . . . . . . . . . iv

- Guide . . . . . . . . . . . . . . . . . . . 1
1 - Numbers 1-5 . . . . . . . . . . . . . . 6
2 - Numbers 6-10 . . . . . . . . . . . . . 18
3 - Shapes . . . . . . . . . . . . . . . . . 30
4 - How Many? . . . . . . . . . . . . . . 42
5 - Addition with Cat and Dog . . . . . . 54

Author Bio . . . . . . . . . . . . . . . . . . . 68

To Every Being--You are much more than just a number

# Guide

I created this math version of my learn-to-read books to bridge the gap between kindergarten math and English. When teaching my kids, I found that a lot of kindergarten math workbooks and worksheets had a lot of words they didn't know and they would get overwhelmed learning all these new words as well as working on the math concepts. So, I've picked some of the common words we encountered when learning kindergarten math and put them in this simple learn-to-read book to hopefully help you and your child make learning to read math words simple and fun!

Combining my background as a homeschooling mother with my knowledge from my Bachelor of Social Work degree, I've taken my personal experiences and mixed that with my understanding of children and the English language to create this series. Each book contains 5 short stories which cover early reading concepts, sight words and vocabulary. A few minutes of your time, your patience and love will go a long way in encouraging success with your new reader. Practicing the sight words (these are simply the common words used in the English language that either are difficult to sound out and/or are so often used that it makes sense to just have them memorized) throughout the day (make a sight word wall, play sight word games, etc) will help your new reader gain mastery over their new reading skills. The accompanying workbook (sold separately) has some helpful worksheets and sight word cut-outs as well for playing sight word games and making a sight word wall.

The purpose behind these learn-to-read books is simple and heartfelt--provide a practical and empowering resource for teaching kids to read. I get it--young kids don't usually like sitting still for long periods of time. Hence, I've curated each of the 5 short story "lessons" in this book to be completed in about 15 minutes following the method I've outlined below. My method shares with you some of the steps I have used (and use) when teaching my kids how to read and had the most success with.

My Method:

1. Pick a story and look through the pages with your child. Observe the illustrations and ask your new reader questions about what they see on the pages. Take your time.
2. Go over the sight word and vocabulary list for the book a few times. Have your child to repeat the words after you if they don't know them.
3. Read the story out loud to your new reader slowly, pointing to each word as you read.
4. Have your new reader try reading the book out loud to you with either you or your child pointing to the words. Offer hints by pointing to the drawings or asking questions and help sound out the words if they are struggling.
5. Have patience, keep practicing and happy reading! Enjoy this beautiful time you get to spend with your new reader!

Tips:
--Hints can be quite helpful. When first having your child read the stories out loud to you themselves, they will likely need some hints. Try pointing to the drawings/part of the drawing the word they are struggling with is referring to (ex. point to the pig if the word they are to read is "pig"). If they are to read the word "like", try prompting with a question such as, "How does Cat feel about the...?" as well as helping sound out the word slowly (lllllllliiiiiii-iikk...). Sometimes, it can be helpful to have your child read the same sentence twice, especially if they needed a lot of help to read it the first time. With it fresh in their mind, they may just be able to go from hardly able to read the sentence to almost reading all the words themselves.

--When YOUR child is ready to learn to read, that is the best time to start teaching them. In other words, don't force it. Whether they are 4 or 7 years old, it doesn't really matter. What matters is that they have that supportive and encouraging person who helps them on their reading journey, whenever the time comes for that to start.

# NUMBERS, SHAPES AND ADDITION — 3

If your child really has no interest, try waiting for a few weeks or even a month or two before trying again. There are lots of other ways to continue teaching some key early reading concepts in the meantime (such as reading out loud to your child) without having a formal "lesson". Relax, get creative and most importantly, have fun! If you're not enjoying the time with your child, chances are they are going to pick up on your energy and meet your lack of enthusiasm with a similar emotion.

--Get their wiggles out first. I've had much more success with my kids being able to focus on the reading lesson when they are well-fed and after they've been physically active. If they are jumping off the walls or have been sitting for a while, try ten minutes of physical activity with them (a great way for everyone to get fit!). A dance party, a workout (check out my kid-friendly workouts online), a short hike or walk around the block, a few races around the house outside or a quick obstacle course are only a few options. Get involved and join in--ten minutes goes by quickly and it's easy to get your heart rate up as well.

--Read lots to your child. Carve out time each day to read age-appropriate books with your child. Take the time to allow them to enjoy the drawings and discuss what you guys see before moving on to reading the words. Point to each word as you read and slowing read the word too. Even if it's the millionth time you've read the story, try to not rush through it. Familiar stories are often one of the best tools for teaching sight words and early reading skills because children start to pick up on the words naturally much like how they learn to comprehend spoken words and start to speak. Perhaps try playing a game with the words when you read. For instance, if your child knows the words "the" and "is", do a quick review of those two words before beginning the story and then tell them that they are going to be in charge of reading those words in the story while you read the other words. With time and practice, particularly with those old favorites, it won't be long before your child is doing most of the reading and you're the one reading the few odd words they haven't mastered (or memorized).

--Words of encouragement go a long way. Try to avoid offering meaningless praise and instead, focus on specific things you noticed (ex. "You really seem to have mastered the sight words "the" and "is"!", "Last time you really struggled with this story but today you barely needed any help at all.").

--Don't forget--teaching your child to read can be a fun and rewarding experience! So relax, get creative and enjoy this wonderful opportunity with your child!

Dear New Reader,

I am so excited that you are starting out on your journey to reading! I created these learn-to-read books with you in mind. It is my hope that these books help you see how fun it is to read and that you realize how capable you are of learning to read. Sometimes there will be challenging moments, but I want you to know that I believe that you can learn to read. More importantly, I hope you believe you can learn to read. With practice and time, you will become a great reader!

In Gratitude,
Erika

# 1
## NUMBERS 1-5

1 2 3 4 5

# NUMBERS, SHAPES AND ADDITION — 7

This is one.

One is blue.

# NUMBERS, SHAPES AND ADDITION — 9

This is two.

Two is red.

This is three.

Three is yellow.

This is four.

Four is green.

This is five.

Five is orange.

## Sight Words

this
is

## Vocabulary

red
blue
yellow
green
orange

# 2
## NUMBERS 6-10

This is six.

Six is pink.

This is seven.

Seven is purple.

This is eight.

Eight is brown.

NUMBERS, SHAPES AND ADDITION  –  25

This is nine.

Nine is gray.

# NUMBERS, SHAPES AND ADDITION – 27

This is ten.

Ten is **black**.

## Sight Words

this
is

## Vocabulary

pink
purple
brown
grey
black

# 3
# SHAPES

# NUMBERS, SHAPES AND ADDITION

This is a circle.

This is a red circle.

This is a square.

This is an orange square.

This is a triangle.

This is a green triangle.

This is a rectangle.

This is a pink rectangle.

This is a star.

This is a blue star.

Sight Words

this
is
a

Vocabulary

circle
blue
triangle
green
square
red
rectangle
yellow
star
purple

# 4

# HOW MANY?

# NUMBERS, SHAPES AND ADDITION – 43

How many birds are there?

I see one bird!

# NUMBERS, SHAPES AND ADDITION — 45

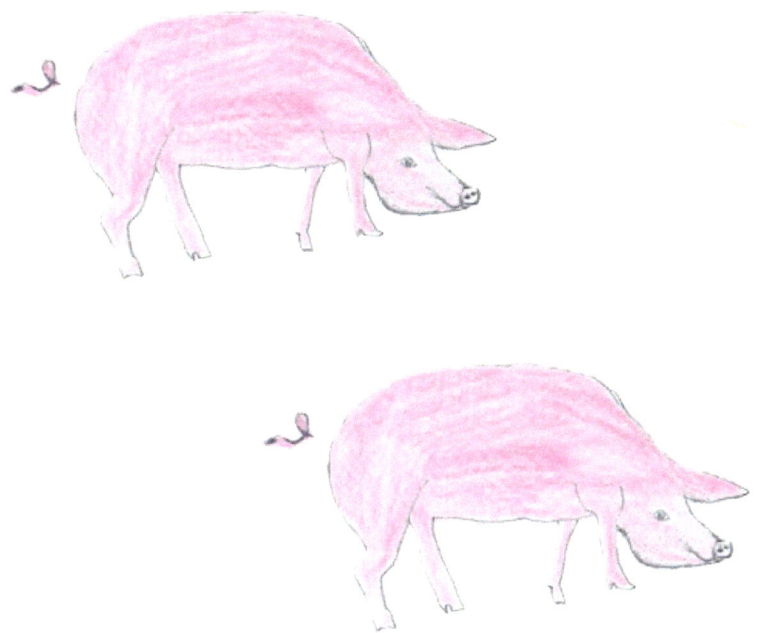

How many pigs are there?

I see two pigs!

How many fish are there?

I see three fish!

# NUMBERS, SHAPES AND ADDITION – 49

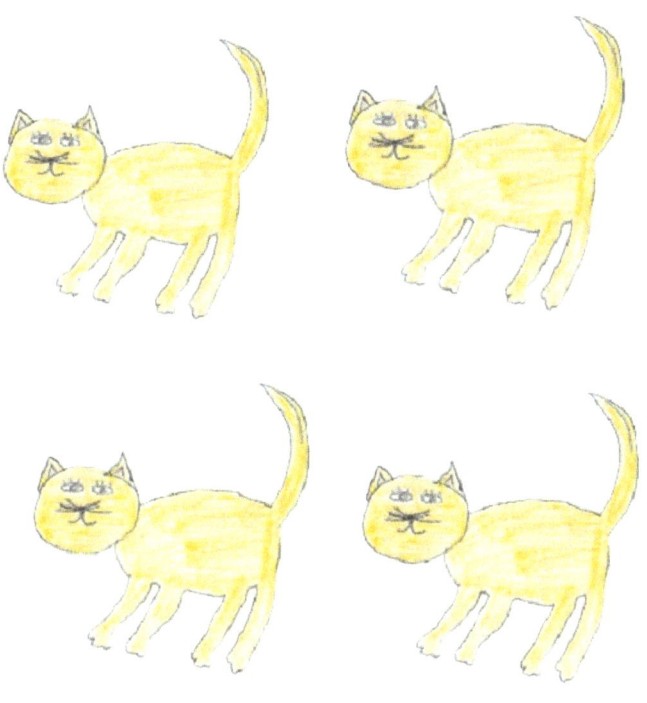

How many cats are there?

I see four cats!

# NUMBERS, SHAPES AND ADDITION – 51

How many dogs are there?

I see 5 dogs!

## Sight Words

how
many
are
there
I
see

## Vocabulary

birds
cats
dogs
fish
pigs

# 5
# ADDITION WITH CAT AND DOG

NUMBERS, SHAPES AND ADDITION  –  55

Cat has one red ball.

Dog has two red balls.

# NUMBERS, SHAPES AND ADDITION – 57

How many red balls do Cat and Dog have altogether?

One plus two equals three.

Cat and Dog have three red balls.

Dog has two green triangles.

# NUMBERS, SHAPES AND ADDITION – 61

Cat has three green triangles.

How many green triangles do Dog and Cat have altogether?

# NUMBERS, SHAPES AND ADDITION – 63

Two plus three equals 5.

Cat and Dog have five green triangles.

## Sight Words

has
many
and
do
have
with
plus
altogether
equals
how

## Vocabulary

cat
one
two
dog
three
five
balls
triangle
red

Composite Sight Word List

a
this
six
and
how
seven
are
equals
eight
at
plus
nine
does
altogether
ten
go
with
is
do
like
have
many
has
not
look
on
one
so

two
three
four
five
there
the
some

# Author Bio

Erika Burton has a Bachelor of Social Work degree and has been educating, raising and caring for children for over 20 years. She is a homeschooling mother and decided to develop these learn-to-read books to assist others in guiding kids on the reading journey. She felt that there needed to be more simple and straightforward books for learning to read after struggling with the resources available when teaching her oldest two kids to read. Her purpose for HALV ROUNDTABLE Learning is from her heart--to provide practical tools for teaching and raising holistically healthy, intelligent and empowered kids.

www.ingramcontent.com/pod-product-compliance
Lightning Source LLC
Chambersburg PA
CBHW041504010526
44118CB00001B/15